Comforts

Bobby Stevenson

"You cannot get through a single day without having an impact on the world around you. What you do makes a difference, and you have to decide what kind of difference you want to make."

Jane Goodall.

TO

To all the love

That died unspoken,

To all the hearts

So quietly broken,

To all the tears

That fell unseen,

To all the things

That might have been.

NEXT YEAR'S LOVE

Next year some people will leave your life

And new ones will enter

Next year some dreams will vanish

And others, not thought of, will come out of the Sun

Next year you'll make mistakes

And you'll survive them all

Next year you'll win some things, and you'll lose some things

Next year some friends will fail to understand

And some will grow to love you

Next year you'll learn a little more about yourself

Some of it you'll like and some of it you won't

Next year perhaps you'll cry alone

But you'll also laugh at things you won't explain to others

Next year some of your actions will be
misunderstood

But you'll discover that others understand in
surprising ways

Next year you'll misjudge hearts and situations

And yet find more caring than you ever thought
possible

Next year you'll learn to love yourself just that little
bit better

And that will be all you'll need.

ALL THE GOOD THINGS

She got up that morning – wondering,
About all the things that made her sad
And all the things that made her mad
So she put them in a big black hat,
Counting...one...two...three....

Then she saw her child and saw her friends,
And that love that she knew would never end,
And she put them in a big white hat,
Counting...one...two...three....

And when she stood and looked at that
The good, the bad and the big tall hats
There were more of all the good things there,
And she had to smile at that.

BEING THERE

To hold the sky from falling on your head,

To make you safe as you dream in your bed,

To stop the World from breaking your heart,

To help you build the most beautiful start,

These are the things I wanted for you,

But being there,

Just being there –

Is the best love I can do.

A BRILLIANT LIFE

Martin was a man. That was the best and the worst of it. He lived in a room that served as his bedroom and sometimes as his kitchen. He had no friends to speak of, but then he had no enemies either.

His parents, Fred and Annie, had high hopes for their boy. They had fought so hard to have a child that when Martin finally did arrive, he was their Moon and stars and Sun.

He had a good heart, and some might say he had the best of hearts.
He tried to be strong for himself and his family, and he made sure he smiled every day, but he did find, as we all do, that there are people in this world who won't let a soul breathe. He didn't judge them too harshly as they had their own reasons. He would simply let the world get him down for a while, pull the covers over his head, and then after sleeping, he would feel better once again.

Martin had his dreams, of course. He'd wanted to be a professional footballer. Then he'd wanted to be a famous actor and other times he'd wanted to sing in front of a million people. After his mother's death, he'd wished he'd been the person who had found the cure for cancer.

Martin never became any of those things, not because he lacked talent but because he felt there were better people than him. Those who knew how good they were, those were the ones that deserved success.

He dreamed of love and being loved, but it never came to be or at least he may have had his eyes closed as it was passing. He watched his school friends grow and marry and have children, and he wished them well and just sometimes, as he sat in the park and saw the parents and their children play, he wished that he were them.

Now don't get me wrong, he wasn't jealous, not for a second, because the world shared out its good and bad and with his parents Martin had the best of all worlds.

Sometimes he wished that he'd had a brother or sister, just someone to visit at Christmas. To have nieces or nephews that he could buy presents and birthday gifts.

Martin saw every single day as a bonus. He wasn't lonely, and he wasn't a loner. He just felt people had better things to do with their time than talk to him.

But he watched the world, and he saw the people and their troubles, and without letting anyone know, he would try to help.

When he had a little drop of extra coins in his life, he would put the money in an envelope and leave it on the step of some deserving door; the lady whose husband who'd left her alone, the child who needed an operation, the man who just wanted a day away from the house.

Martin wasn't a saint, not by any stretch of the imagination. Martin had hurt people, and he'd wasted opportunities, and most importantly, he'd wasted time.

Because we all have our own ideas of what sin is, but to Martin, wasting time was up there with the big ones.

He sent Christmas and Valentine cards to the lonely souls in the street. He sent postcards to the old lady who, like him, had no family. She probably didn't know who or where it came from, but the important thing was that someone had written to her.

You see, none of what he did was ever significant, but it mattered to the people he helped. This world is awash with lonely souls, and to someone like Martin who could appreciate that point, he felt it was his place to do something about it. Martin's gone now, and I'm not sure if he moved or just closed his eyes for the last time.

No one noticed that there was no longer a light on in Martin's house, but they did notice there were no longer little gifts on the doorstep or that cards were no longer being sent.

Martin had accepted that what he had been given in his life was his life, and he had used it all in the best ways he could.

He sometimes smiled, he sometimes cried, and he nearly always laughed.

LOVE YOURSELF

When you look in the mirror, love yourself.
When you do something good, love yourself.
When you do something bad, love yourself,
Just tell yourself not to do it again.
When someone loves you, let them.
When someone hates you, let them,
Doesn't matter because you love yourself.
You're made up of atoms flung together by science
or a god.
So when you don't love yourself,
Who will?
Always, always, love yourself.

A SIMPLE TRUTH

"You get to every day by winning, you know that
don't you?" Was what she used to say to us kids
when we'd taken a tumble or were feeling really
low.
"So don't you be telling me you failed, or nothing
as stupid as that," she'd say, just before she'd give
you a smile that could span an ocean.

"You ain't done wrong and you ain't let anyone
down and don't let me hear you say you have –
'cause you ain't. To get here, to this moment
where we are stood, you must have fought a
million and one battles – and.........AND......," she'd
say twice just so's you'd have to listen, then she'd
shake her big pointy finger straight at your face:
"AND...not only have you fought all those goddamn
fights, but you must have won them all, or else you
wouldn't be here standing in front of little old me.
Now ain't I right, or ain't I right?"

Then she'd shuffle in her slippers to the little room
where she kept the whiskey - and as she shuffled,
she'd holler and laugh all the way there. If you
were here, you were winning. Simple as that.
I can still hear her now after all these years - and
you know what? I'm still winning.

WHY I MENTION YOUR NAME

I know you wonder from that place you stand,

In the far undiscovered country,

Why I mention your name so often,

In conversations, in stories, in laughter, and in hopes,

It's because I know that a person dies twice,

Once when their heart stops beating,

And the second time,

When someone mentions their name,

For the very last time.

TODAY IS GOING TO BE A GREAT DAY

"Today is going to be a great day," said the little boy

Whose mother unexpectedly opened her eyes

Today is going to be a great day, smiled the old man

As the pain in his hands stopped for a time

Today is going to be a great day, laughed the young mum

As she picked up the money from the street

Today is going to be a great day, thought the doctor

As he put the diamond ring back in his pocket

Ready for the big question

Today is going to be a great day, chuckled the large man

At the bus stop, with the Sun on his face

Who was just happy to be alive,

Today was going to be a great day, after all.

I'M WAITING FOR THE WINDS TO BLOW

I'm waiting for the winds to blow,

And someday soon, or later,

They'll take me on a voyage,

To a land of somewhere greater.

And if we do not get the chance

To wish ourselves goodbye,

I'll look for you in kinder places,

As I go sailing by.

BE HAPPY

Be happy, I mean it.

One day what you thought were troubles

Will only be a piece of grit in the ointment.

Be happy now.

Honestly, what you think of as problems

Are only because the rest of your

Life is working out.

You can't have everything all the time.

Be happy. Smile. Be strong.

One day something else will own your smile.

Be happy now.

WE NEED YOUR HEART TO SING ITS SONG

Don't cry too long

My little one

The world is waiting on your smile

Don't listen to the midnight whispers

It is their way

To make things dark

Don't feel

That other hearts are hardened

Sometimes they need

To take a rest

Don't wish that you were someone

Other

This life is only meant to test.

Don't think

That you are somehow chosen

For all the trials in the world

Don't cry too long

My little urchin

We need your heart to sing

Its song.

HOW I WAS

It was only a few short summers between my
mother asking,

'how I was' and her asking 'who I was'.

It was only the briefest of moments between
telling a friend,

'See you soon' and bowing my head in a farewell.

It seems only days between being a child and
looking after one,

Between laughing and shouting, 'I'm old' and being
old.

Surely the Moon has only passed a few times since
saying

'tomorrow, I'm going to..' and 'yesterday, I meant
to....'

It has only been a few short, warm-wind summers
since my mother asked me how I was.

THE PROMISE

When you fall, I will catch you,

When you call, I will be there,

When you stumble, I will lift you,

When you're drowning, give you air,

When you hurt, then I will hold you,

When you break, I'll make you whole,

When you're down, I'll make you smile,

When you're lost, I'll be your goal,

When you're weak, I'll make the world turn,

When you lose faith, I'll be strong,

When you doubt, I'll be your beacon,

I will love you all lifelong.

ONE DAY WHEN YOU LEAST EXPECT IT

The stand-up and be glorious thing about it is:

You'll never know when or how it happens,

Never know what effect you've had,

Or who you've saved.

It might be the smile to a passing stranger,

Who was on their way to shout at someone –

A someone who would have driven home in anger,

And didn't see the person they knocked over.

Or a face on a train,

The one who was going to get off at the next lonely station

And jump.

But you helped them with their coat, or hat, or bag,

And they saw a warmth in life again.

Perhaps you held the door open for a soul who then

Held the door open for a stranger, who changed
their mind,

About pulling the trigger.

One day, when you least expect it,

You will change the world,

And you will probably never, ever know.

TO FILL A HUMAN HEART

To fill a human soul,
Takes strength and smiles,
To fill a human head,
Takes wisdom and time,
To fill a human life,
Takes courage and hope,
But to fill a human heart,
Takes love,
Takes love.

To fill a lifetime lived,
Takes all that we have,
To fill a child with hope,
Takes kindness and patience,
To fill a lover's dreams,
Takes selfless devotion,
But to fill a human heart,
Takes everything.

IF ALL OF THIS WERE UP TO ME

If all of this were up to me,

My gifts would be of other things,

The son to spend an afternoon

With a father long since gone,

The granddad seeing his offspring grow,

 As his life goes on and on,

The children gone before their time,

Would come back home and ring the chime,

And chances lost would be our choice,

To try just one more time,

The girl whose births would fill a home,

A brother not a day alone,

The friend who'd never know the pain,

Of all that cancer brings,

If all of this were up to me, then these would be my things.

THE BEST OF ALL SUMMERS

Some things remain with you forever.

When I was ten years old, my father took me on a trip in an old, battered car and caravan, and although I didn't know it at the time, my father was dying. He was only forty years of age, and he was dying of a brain tumour.

What can I tell you about me back then? That I was the only son of parents who never got around to marrying? That I lived with my two sisters and a cat and that despite not having any money, we lived in a house packed to the roof with love.

Maybe that's as good as it gets in anyone's life. My father was the gentlest of hearts and the kindest of men, and I'm not just saying that because he's gone. I'm saying it because it was true. It was his strength and his weakness. My mother watched so many people taking advantage of his goodness that, in the end, she put herself in the way of anyone trying to use him. This made her seem hard, but she was willing to put up with that because that was what our family was always about – love.

My parents had decided that when school was closed for the summer, Mum and the girls would go to London for a few days to see a show, while me and Dad would go north taking his old car hooked up to Granddad's caravan. I knew Dad was probably hoping this would be a chance for us to talk, as he was always working, and I was always in my bedroom being misunderstood. Even at ten years of age, I had no real idea how to enjoy myself.

On that summer, that glorious summer, school finished, and my life began. Dad drove Mum and the girls to the railway station, and I sat on the front steps waiting, bag ready and caravan packed.

I'll always remember the 'toot-toot-toot' of my Dad on the car horn as he returned from the station, letting everyone in the street know that the boys were off on holiday. All those unused days were spread before us, waiting.

If I'd thought that it was going to be a particularly difficult time sitting in the car with my Dad, I was wrong. I had imagined him and me struggling to talk to each other and stumbling over words. I guess I've always made assumptions about things. I've worried and assumed – I suppose that's what should be written on my headstone. There I go again.

As we drove towards the coast, I felt ashamed of myself. Here was a man who knew all about my writings and about the books I'd read. He would steal himself into my room after he came home late from work, too late to wish me goodnight but long enough to kiss me on the forehead and absorb from the room who and what I was. There was I knowing very little about him, except he was my father, and he was rarely home.

I don't recall when he stopped the car, but I do remember it getting dark. I had been telling him all about the characters in some Dickens novel when I must have fallen asleep in his arms. When I awoke, it was morning, and the Sun was fighting the condensation on the window. Dad had placed me in the back seat and covered me with his jacket.

The car was freezing, and as I sat up, I shivered. I wiped away mist from the side window and saw that despite the Sun, the sky and the sea were a cold blue, broken up by the foamy edges of the waves. We had parked at the edge of a cliff, and Dad was sitting, staring – that was all he was doing – just staring. When I felt brave enough, I ventured outside to join him. I'll always remember his face that day, the wind had slapped his cheeks into a Santa Claus red, and his eyes were watering, stung by the sea. You could almost imagine that he had been crying, and I wonder now, from all those years away, if he had been.

He told me to sit next to him, and he put his arm around me, "You and me, son, are going on an adventure".

Now don't get me wrong, I liked the sound of 'adventure', and I loved my father and felt safe with him, but there was always a part of me that wanted to return to the protection of my bedroom, pull up my arms into my sleeves and wait on the next hurtful thing. Yeah, you're right. I was one weird kid.

As we came over the hill, I could see it: Blackpool Tower. I had never seen anything so tall in all my life and was so excited that I forgot about my misgivings. The place was alive with people who were swept up with enjoying life and buzzing with laughter. There were donkey rides by the sea, the odd uncle with a handkerchief on his head to keep the Sun away, and people breaking their teeth on sticks of rocks, slurping ice cream and getting pieces of candy floss stuck to their noses.

Dad and I went down on to the beach and ate our fish and chips from a newspaper. I think it was the best fish and chips I ever tasted.

"That's better," said Dad.

"What?"

"You're smiling. You've got a nice smile, you know. You should use it more often."

"Oh, Dad."

"I'm just saying."

And do you know what? I felt that I didn't want to be anywhere else. Just me and my Dad on the beach at Blackpool.

"It's my fault," he said sadly.

"What is, Dad?"

"The fact that you never smile, me and your Mum left you sitting too long in that room of yours."
"I like my room."
"No one likes their room."

Dad parked the caravan down some quiet side street and told me to get washed and ready as he took a walk into town. When he returned, his breath smelt of beer and his clothes of cigarettes. "You'll never guess what I've got in my pocket? Two tickets to see Arthur Askey at the Grand".

What a night that was, everyone, laughing and singing along with The Bee Song. I looked over at my Dad, and he was laughing so hard the tears were rolling down his face. God, I miss him.

We had ice cream topped with raspberry sauce on the way back, and I never once thought about my misgivings, not once.

The next morning after a cup of tea and a bacon roll, we left Blackpool still singing the Bee Song, just me and my Dad.

I can't remember who saw the old lady first. My Dad had stopped the car because I needed to pee again, and I was hiding in the bushes. The woman was sitting on a bench, and at first, we thought she was just sleeping, but her head had rolled forwards, and she was moaning. Dad put his ear

close to listen to her breathing.
"This isn't good. We'll need to get her to hospital."

I sat with her in the back seat of the car while she rested her head on my lap. She reminded me of my Gran. I almost said, "We won't be long now, Gran," when she moaned loudly. The nurse brought Dad and me drinks as we sat in the corridor waiting on news. It almost felt like it was my Gran.
"Are you family?"
Dad explained to the doctor that we had found her sitting by the side of the road.

"There was nothing we could do, I'm afraid. I'm sorry your trip was in vain. She passed away five minutes ago."

Dad got a bit annoyed, but he kept it to himself until we were outside the hospital. I thought maybe he was sad about the old lady dying, but really he was a bit angry.
"Don't you ever believe that what we did was in vain, son. Never think that. That poor lady would have died alone on that bench if we hadn't stopped. As it is, you kept her company, and there were people with her when she went. So, it wasn't in vain. Nothing is in vain. Always, always remember that. Everything matters".

I guess that's the kind of thing that happens to a person when they come out of their room.

As Dad drove north, I had the feeling that he just
wanted to keep driving, but as soon as it started to
get dark, we stopped. Thinking back, I guess he
couldn't see too well in the dying light, something
to do with his tumour. We set the caravan down in
a field that overlooked Liverpool. What a city.

I loved the way that the setting sun painted the
building tops a crimson yellow. We were going into
town tomorrow, and Dad said he had a surprise.
I don't think I have ever been to a happier city than
Liverpool that day.

People were going to and fro but always laughing
and joking. Some were singing, others whistling. I
loved every minute of it, every blooming minute of
it.

"I've got a pal, and he owes me a favour", said Dad.
I felt ashamed that I hadn't even known that my
father had any friends or who they were.
"He works at a club down Matthew Street. He says
if we arrive early enough, he'll get us in, and you
can hide under my coat."

I almost had misgivings again, almost wishing I
were back in my safe, warm bedroom – almost.

We did what Dad said, and he put me under his
coat and the doorman, his pal, waved us past all
the people waiting to get in.
"We'll need to keep you undercover young 'un,"

said Bert, Dad's pal, as he led me to a small room
by the stairs where he gave me lemonade.
"We'll come and get you when the band is ready,"
said my Dad. "I'm going to have a talk with Bert.
You'll be okay here?"
I would be.

I had just finished my drink when there was a
knock at the door, followed by it opening.
"Hey Paul, look what I've found, the Cavern has
little people living under the stairs. What are you
doing here, son?"
I told him I was waiting on the band and that my
Dad was coming to get me.
"And what band would that be, son?"

I shrugged, and the man seemed to find that funny.
His pal, Paul, came over to have a look at me.
"You're right, John, that is one of the little people.
You've got to be lucky to see them," and then he
rubbed my head.

John said it was his band that was playing, and I
said I was sorry. He said not as sorry as he was and
asked did I want to come to their dressing room?
Although on second thoughts, John said, there was
probably more room under the stairs.

So, I went with John and Paul and met the other
two, George and Pete. They were all fooling around
and didn't seem to be in any way nervous. John

asked me what I wanted to do. "That is when you stop being one of the little people."

I told him I wanted to be a writer, and he said that was probably the best job in the world next to being in a band, especially his band, and he went into his jacket and gave me his pen.
"If anyone asks, tell them John Lennon gave it to you."

That night I watched John, Paul, George and Pete play the most wonderful music I had ever heard or will ever hear. I didn't know it then, but a few weeks later, Ringo replaced Pete. I never got to meet him.
My Dad died, just after Christmas, that year.

He left me with the best present that I have ever received in my life. He took me out of my room and locked the door so that I couldn't go back in. So, what if I got hurt? That was the price you paid for being out there, that was the price we all paid, and the other thing he gave me was the belief that nothing is ever in vain, nothing.

On the thirtieth anniversary of John Lennon's death, I flew to New York and walked through Central Park and climbed the hill to Strawberry Fields.

There was a little boy about ten and his Dad listening to the music of Lennon, and I took out the pen, and I handed it to them:

"John Lennon gave me this."
Everything matters.

THE FIRST TIME

The first time you do it,

The first time you don't ask or seek permission,

And you just are,

The first time you take off those sunglasses,

When you've been told all your life who and what
you are,

Is scary, and strange, and wonderful.

The first time you don't look for opinions or
wonder if you are right,

Is the first day of the rest of your life.

And me?

Well, I am ashamed that it took me so long,

But here's to all your first times.

Everyone.

I WISH I HAD FALLEN MORE

I wish I had fallen more,

It would have shown I was trying harder than I should,

I wished I had pushed more doors open, cried more often,

Listened more, started more fights, started more smiles,

Made more friends, held more people,

Dried more tears, caused more fun.

Wished I had laughed more,

Until the pee ran down my leg,

I wished I had said 'sorry' more,

Talked to more hearts,

Wished I had fallen more,

Got rejected by more strangers,

It would have shown I was trying,

Wished I had failed more,

It would have meant I was alive,

I just wish I had fallen more.

RUN. LIVE. ASAP.

Run my friend and don't look back
Don't think the rest of life is yours
Or that unfinished day
Will hold its course as planned
Take what you think is needed now
Don't hesitate, for loss is never reinstated
Breathe deep and strong
Then run and love and live
And tell all of those who need to know
How much their hearts are needed.

BE WHO YOU ARE

Be who you are,

Be magnificent,

Be strong,

And except to those who cared too much,

The one who never quite belonged.

Be who you are,

Stand tall, unique

Be grand

The one who smiled at little jokes,

That no one else could understand.

Be who you are,

Let laughter roll the same as tears

Take pleasure in the here and now,

Not in the days or months, or years.

Be who you are,

Be loved

And loving everything,

Don't back away from chance nor dare,

You, too, will have your song to sing.

Be who you are,

Let happiness and joy

Break through,

The Universe was wise enough to only make the one of you.

THANK YOU FOR TODAY

Thank you for today,

Not everything was good,

But then not everything was bad,

I woke up sad and somewhere in the sunshine

The day got a little better.

Thank you for today,

For letting me see that

Life is difficult for every heart

And some things, which I find easy, others don't

And I know the opposite is true

Thank you for today,

And although I am not where I want to be

I realise that I might just get

To where I'm meant to be, one day.

Thank you for today,

Thank you for today,

For although I never felt like I was a winner

I managed to scrape my way through it all

And learned to hide the disappointments

Thank you for today

Seriously.

THE MAN WHO LIVED TWICE

There was a story from the early 1950s in Glasgow about Sammy, a man who used to play the violin. Sammy didn't have a home, but sometimes a kind soul would let him rest his head on their sofa or in their garden shed.

In those days, people used to queue outside the movie theatres awaiting the start of the film, if it were a rainy night – and in Glasgow that was almost a certainty – people were cold and bored, and this is where Sammy would find his audience. Up and down the queue, he'd play old ones, new ones, tunes from the war and tunes from the dance halls. Kind folks would throw a penny or two into Sammy's hat; he'd nod with a thank you and move up the queue. Folks were glad to see old Sammy, and it all felt part of their night's entertainment.

When the building had swallowed up the audience for the last show, Sammy would tip the contents of his hat into his pocket and head off to the Coronation Café for a cup of tea and his first food of the day. On good days he might have a cake to follow. This particular day had been a good day, and he'd made seven shillings and three pence. Two shillings of this would go into a box he kept hidden for the days when he didn't feel too good and couldn't make it to the cinema.

If he didn't have anywhere rest his head that

evening, Sammy liked nothing better than to sit in the café and talk with friends and strangers – about this and that and everything else in between. Sammy had lots of favourite topics; one was about God and his place in the Universe.

"There can only be two theories on the universe, either there is a God, and all of this is a reflection of his personality, or this is a universe without a driver, and it is all the more wonderful for that," Sammy would say with a wicked glint in his eye.

But people didn't really listen to an old man who played the violin in a cinema queue. I mean, what would someone like that know?
The other things Sammy liked to discuss were his belief that one day soon, "before I die," he would say, "we will see a man walking on the moon." And the second, a big topic with him, was that television would quickly take over the world.

Friends and strangers would laugh at the outrageous things he said. After all, he was an old tramp who knew nothing.

One night, one cold rainy night, when ironically the people were queuing to see Singing In The Rain, Sammy found that the queue was so large there was little room for him to move up and down, so he had to step on to the road, and that was when it happened – the number 59 bus hit Sammy full on.

Some folks thought he had died right there and then, but he'd only bumped his head on the way down and had passed out. Naturally, they took him to the hospital, where he spent several comfortable and warm nights. It even went through Sammy's head that perhaps he should make jumping in front of a bus a regular occurrence.

A big chief from the bus company came to see Sammy in the hospital, probably just to see what the damage was. "You shouldn't have been on the road. You understand it was your fault," said the big chief. But the truth of the matter was that some of the people in the queue said that Sammy had been pushed into the road and that the bus was going too fast, especially on a wet and windy night.

"So, taking all factors into account, we have decided to give you this," said the chief and handed Sammy a cheque for £150. Sammy asked if it was okay to have it in real money instead, as he didn't have a bank account. The chief sent over his secretary with the money to the hospital the following night.

Between the money that Sammy had in his box and some of the money the bus company gave him, Sammy bought himself a little caravan and a place to put it. For the first time in many years, he had a permanent roof over his head and some money to feed himself.

He didn't waste the cash. Instead, he bought himself a rather smart suit from Woolworth and on the first night out he wore it, he noticed a significant change in people. Folks walking along Argyle Street would say hello to him or nod or wish him well. After all, he was a smartly dressed man, and so he had to be one of their own.

He decided to use some of his money and watch a classical music concert in a big hall on Bath Street. at first hearing, and when he talked to some of the performers afterwards, they suggested that if he loved to play the violin, why didn't he come along to their rehearsals on a Thursday.

After the first Thursday he attended, Sammy was asked to join the orchestra, which made him happier than he had ever been before.
After practice, the gang, as Sammy called them, would go to a late-night café bar and discuss this and that and everything in between.

When Sammy told them about his thoughts on the Universe and the Moon and television, they sat enthralled listening to this well dressed, talented man with so much genius in his head.

Wasn't he the cleverest, most talented man they had ever met?

ONE DAY, MY FRIEND, WE'LL SOAR

One day, my friend, we'll soar,

Far, high above these streets of darkened hearts,

We'll tilt our wings to freedom,

And scrape the highest of the skies.

One day, my friend, we'll soar,

Up there, all wrapped in splendid sunlight,

Riding azure blue jet streams,

Breathless with that rush of life and air.

One day, my friend, we'll soar,

So let me take your broken body upon my back,

And both of us shall climb in painless flight,

I'll let you rest up there, but promise I'll be back.

JUST 'CAUSE YOU'RE BREATHING

Just 'cause you're breathing,

Doesn't mean you're alive,

Just 'cause you're clever,

Doesn't mean that you're wise,

Just 'cause you've faith,

Doesn't mean that you're kind,

Because you can see,

Doesn't mean you're not blind.

Just 'cause you're loving,

Doesn't mean you know love,

And by sitting in church,

You don't speak for Above,

Just 'cause you're hurting,

Doesn't make you unique,

And because you feel down,

Doesn't mean that you're weak,

Just 'cause you're thinking,

Doesn't mean you don't strive,

Just 'cause you're breathing,

Doesn't mean you're alive.

ONE DAY, I PASSED PERFECTION

The smell of shoe polish and summer,

The taste of dandelion and burdock lemonade,

The Sun as rosy, red as it ever was,

My Grandmother's arm around me

Kissing the top of my head,

The days of leaving home for school

Knowing everyone who mattered would still be there.

The Beano and Dandy on a Thursday,

Man from Uncle and Top of The Pops.

One day,

A long, long time ago,

I quietly passed perfection

And didn't even notice.

SKIING IN CENTRAL PARK

I don't think there was a precise time when you could say that they actually met; instead, it would be more accurate to say that they rubbed against each other's lives from the moment they were born.

Kitty and Jethro were born in the same week to families who lived next door to each other. They grew up together, sat in the same school rooms, and had the same good and bad teachers.

When one of them missed school due to ill health, the other couldn't rest until they were back together.

It was inevitable that one day they would start to see each other in a different light. One evening Jethro looked at Kitty and saw not a little friend who needed to be rescued but a beautiful young girl who needed to be held. And one summer's day, instead of a little boy who always needed his nose wiped or his tears dried, Kitty saw a strong, upstanding boy who she could think of perhaps marrying one day.

Jethro spent a long time away in the army when the government felt that he was needed, and in those times apart (it seems strange to anyone who has not experienced it), she fell more in love with him than she could put into words.

Their wedding was in the little chapel just north of the town's river, and everyone turned up – it was said that the sheriff allowed his prisoners to attend and even 'though the sheriff got real drunk that night, the prisoners locked themselves up, afterwards.

The two love birds settled down to a life in the little town that was bypassed by all the main roads, and there they got on with the business of living.

When no kids turned up, Kitty went to the doctor and found that she and Jethro just weren't compatible – had it been with someone else, both might have had children, but not in this combination. Kitty knew things could have been done to help them, but they both decided that if that was the way things were, then they just get on with it.

Not having younger ones to worry about meant they got to see a lot of the country. They drove north, south, east, and west and loved every single minute of every single day in each other's company.

There was one crazy dream that they both shared (Kitty thinks she first read about it in a book), and it was their wish to go skiing in Central Park in New York City. Neither of them had ever been to another country, but this seemed the perfect reason to go. They knew there were only the smallest of hills in the park, but that didn't put either of them off – not one bit. Every winter, they would talk about going to New York, and then before they knew it, another year had passed. They were in their sixties when Jethro started to get ill, and it meant that Kitty spent more and more time looking after him. It wasn't a chore; she just worried about her little boy who had once lived next door to her. One winter, just before the start of December, Jethro shut his eyes for the last time. When Kitty found herself brave enough, she started to sort out Jethro's things. In an old jacket, she found details about a savings account in the little bank at the top of the street.

When she went into the bank, the young man behind the counter said:

"So you're going skiing in New York, then?" Kitty asked him what he meant, and he told her that every week, Jethro had put a little money into the skiing account and that one day, he told him, Jethro and his wife were going to go skiing in Central Park. Kitty counted the money, and there was enough to get her to fly to New York and a little over to help a young family who lived next door. When she got to New York, it was September, in fact, the hottest month since records began – so skiing was out the question.

That night she sat in her hotel room and talked to Jethro as she always did, and after telling him she hoped he was well wherever he was, she mentioned the lack of snow. It was then that a TV show came on about the Guggenheim Museum in New York and gave her an idea.

The next day she took a cab to the museum where the security man at the door looked in her bag – she told him 'they were for her grand-kids', so he wished her a pleasant visit, and Kitty went on her way.

When she looked up, it was just as she had hoped – the inside of the Guggenheim was a path which descended from the top of the building to the bottom, in circles. She got on an elevator to the top floor, took out her new roller-skates and before anyone could stop her, she shot down the Guggenheim path at several miles per hour.

"Can you see me, Jethro?" Kitty shouted, "can you see what I'm doing?"

And then she laughed and giggled and screamed all the way to the bottom of the path.

ONE DAY

One day when this journey's ended,
When the sun is setting low,
You'll come for me and wait for me,
Where the wild blue waters flow.

One day when I'm old and tired,
When this life is almost through,
You'll lift me up and carry me,
To the peace that we once knew.

One day when the heartache's over,
When the tears no longer come,
You'll whisper softly in my ear,
My love,
My love,
Come home.

KEEP GOING FOR ALL THE REASONS YOU TELL OTHERS

You'll make it. I know you will,

You've come too far, and now is not the time.

If you only stopped and thought about it all

The walls you've climbed, all the troubles crossed

All the failures faced, all the little victories

So that one day soon, you'll make it across

To where you can start again

I know you will

You've come too far to stop.

REST

I know you're tired of that twisted road,

Tired of climbing those hills,

Tired of getting to the top of one,

Only to have to drop down into another valley,

So why not just kick off those dusty shoes,

And sit with me a while,

No need to talk,

Come listen to the birds sing,

Feel the Sun on your face,

Or the rain in your hair,

Know that we are sitting next to each other,

Neither of us is the enemy,

We are both only trying to keep going,

Remembering that some days are harder than others,

It's life that we are both battling,

So, close your eyes, breathe in gently,

And know that we will both get back on the road again,

In a while.

BORN BEAUTIFUL

You were born beautiful, and boy did the Universe work to get you here.

You were born with the potential for a million things.

But on the day you wanted to paint a picture, you were busy.

On the day you could have shown the world how you were at football,

You had to keep someone else happy.

On the day you could have reached across to your soul mate,

You were going through something or other.

You were born beautiful, and when they buried you,

Most of what you never did was buried with you.

SUNSHINE

Tread lightly with those souls who bring tears,

Walk proudly with those hearts divine,

Stand tall with folks whose smiles are proudest,

Stand close to those who bring the sunshine.

Don't share a path with folks who turn the lights down,

Who bathe their way in darkness all the time,

Be brave with those who make your hearts smile,

Stand close to those who bring the sunshine.

NEVER LOSE HOPE

They'll be dark days and sunny ones,

Happy and frightening ones,

Sad and alone ones,

But never lose hope.

They'll be surprising and scary ones,

Days when there's nothing done,

Days when your heart's gone,

Yet never lose hope,

For they'll be good days and great days,

And can't-do-no wrong days,

Everything's going my way,

Please never lose hope.

ON SOME QUIET SMILING DAY

I know nothing of the rules you use,

Or the gods,

Or stars you live by

All I know is how I've done,

How I've kept,

My peace within,

I've never been the best of men,

And many times, I've failed in all I was.

But on some quiet, smiling day,

I've tried to help,

And telling no one,

Leave something,

Better than it's found.

I know nothing of the buildings that you pray in,

Or the books you live through,

All I know is I try to be kind

To be decent, to understand,

To care.

Sometimes that is not enough,

I know.

But I'll never stop trying.

WE WALKED A PATH ONCE

We walked a path once,

You and I,

And shared some gentle time while basking in the Sun,

We walked a road once,

You and I,

Fighting with the storms that blew upon our way,

We walked a highway once,

You and I,

And dealt with all the loss and hurt that fell before us,

We walked the Earth once,

You and I,

And broke with everything that Heaven threw in our direction,

But now the time has come for the parting of the ways,

And you will take one path, and I will hold the other,

And we will walk the Universe,

You and I,

But with other souls as company.

THE NEXT TIME

The next time, I'll say 'hi' when that moment first arises

The next time, I'll cross the street before the trouble starts

The next time, I won't put the money on that horse that cost me everything

The next time, I'll go with whom I love rather than who you said I should

The next time, I will tell you that I'm unhappy and not just smile through gritted teeth

The next time, I'll live the way I want to and not because I am scared

The next time, I won't let them hit me or call me names

The next time, I will not wait so long

The next time, I'll take that chance

The next time, I will not throw away friends and money like that

The next time, I'll make sure they're properly dead

The next time, I'll take my share as well

The next time, I will not drink as much

The next time, I will not hit you, I promise

The next time, I'll be the one to stay on the path and make you move

The next time, I'll spend more time talking and listening

The next time, I'll be far gentler on myself and my life

The next time, I'll probably do it all again, just like the last time.

DANCING TO THE MUSIC OF MY HEART

I never picked a proper tune to dance to

And I never got in step with any goal

And in all those dancing years

I spent wishing I could hear

That melody which drove another's soul

I guess it's too late now to ever

Try and change things

As I'm nearing my own moment to depart

So, I'll quietly spend the time

That's been allocated mine

Dancing to the music of my heart.

I WILL REMEMBER YOU

I will remember you when the best of you has gone

I will remember you when the song you loved is sung

I will remember you when I stand on hills where we once walked

I will remember you and your laughter as we talked

I will remember you and all the kindness that was shown

I will remember you when your tired soul has flown

I will remember you when each new day has a dawn

I will remember you when the last of you has gone

THE GREATEST KISS

You stood there on the hill, looking down at the
town,
Thinking of all the things that had gone wrong,
All the little dreams that had turned to smoke.
"Why me?" Was all you could think of.
"Why them?" Was what got you the most.
Then that thought came to you
And a little bit of warmth hit your smile.
Because the day of your greatest kiss still lay ahead
And that was forever worth holding on for.

ALL I ASK OF TODAY

Give me the strength to just get through today

To deal with this day's concerns and nothing more

Give me the courage to see it through to the end

And don't let me be blinded by my struggles

Let me see the goodness in people and in those
who care

Give me the strength to deal with today's fears

And let tomorrow take care of itself

Give me the heart to lend a helping hand to others

As I pull myself up.

Please just give me the strength to get through
today

And nothing more is all I ask.

IF YOU SHOULD EVER NEED ME

If you should ever need me

And find that I'm not there

Look for me in happy eyes

And hearts that want to share

If you should ever want me

Just whisper out my name

For I will always watch for you

And help you with your pain

If you should ever need me

And find that I'm not there

You'll catch me in the shadows

Always ready to take care.

THE TROUBLE IS YOU THINK YOU HAVE TIME

You think you have time,

To be annoyed, or to be angry,

To not speak, or not call.

You think you have time,

To work up the courage to say hello,

Or tell the one you want that you love them.

You think you have time,

To consider this, or ponder that,

Or shrug and say, next week I will,

You think you have time,

To return a long-lost kindness,

Or make a long-held deal.

You think you have time,

To begin to learn to love yourself,

And to cease the worrying in your heart,

But you don't,

And you won't,

And you probably never will.

Because you see, you think you have time.....

MY FAVOURITE THOUGHT

You are my favourite thought, favourite smile,
favourite life,

You're my first thing in the morning and my last
thing at night,

When I speak to other souls, it is you in my head,

I long for you beside me, I dream of you in bed.

You are my favourite thought, favourite day,
favourite night,

When I stumble through the darkness, you carry
the light.

No one can fathom this smile on my face,

It is you – it is you, who makes my heart race.

You are my favourite thought, favourite deed,
favourite one,

You are my Moon and my stars and my Sun,

You are the body where my dreams have been
caught,

You are my love, my favourite thought.

YOUR STORY HASN'T ENDED

No matter how low you think you've dropped

Your story hasn't ended

No matter how far your path has gone

Your story hasn't ended

No matter how sad your heart can feel

Your story hasn't ended

No matter how long it takes to get you there

Your story hasn't ended.

LEARN TO CLIMB TREES

Learn to climb trees,

And live with skinned knees,

Learn to jump gaps and laugh,

Learn to handstand,

Play a tune, join a band,

Learn to tap dance in the bath.

Learn to be foolish,

And live without care,

Learn to sing songs and cry,

Learn your name in Swahili,

And learn to climb trees,

And never stop asking 'why?'

HEARTBEATS

There's a finite number of heartbeats

To each and every life

Some less than some would hope for

Some more than some would like

Yet every beat's a milestone

Which flags that one more's spent

And nothing can retrieve them

From that far place

Where they went.

THE MORNING OF THE DAY

She could feel the Sun on her heart as its rays broke through the window. There was a bird, a blackbird, singing in the old, twisted trees. She heard the cyclists from the city shouting to one another as their bikes sailed past her front door.

The aroma of the freshly made coffee had skipped the stairs and had, instead, entered her room through a little opened window.

There was a quiet tap as a bee kept hitting on her glass pane, looking for somewhere new to live. Then without warning, the heat started to bubble through her veins, and pumped her lips and brightened her eyes. No longer did her heart skip a beat. It was like an engine, blasting a way forward.

She had done with the dull days, and the rain, and the mist that had arrived with the darkness. She had done with avoiding mirrors and reflections. She was finished with treating herself as the enemy and listening to others' sourness: their paths were their problems and responsibilities.

She sat up in bed, smiled for the first time in a long time, and decided it was the day to be happy again.

ONCE UPON A LONG AGO

Once upon, a long ago,
I saw a life of hope
And so,
I dreamed myself with smile
And mirth,
A charming life to death, from birth
But living twisted all I did
The rules were changed,
My fortunes hid,
I wish my days had run just so,
Like once upon,
A long ago.

STAND UP TO CANCER

No one will stand by your grave and weep
Nor will they talk of long-lost friends
No one will raise a drink nor wish you well
For all the years you spent nearby
You were not asked, nor were you wanted here
Be sure you have not won the War
This battle has only just begun
We will not rest, nor disappear
Until the day a child asks: "Please tell me, what was cancer?"

WHEN IT'S TIME FOR YOU TO GO

When it's time for you to go,

Don't turn and wave,

Instead,

Consider this,

If there should be a blessed place,

Beyond,

A land of half-forgotten ghosts,

Then I will follow you and

We shall meet once more,

But if this other Eden,

Should prove unformed,

Remember this,

One day, I too will rest among

The longest sleep,

And you, alone, no more.

THE STARS WANTED HER BACK

When I first got to know her,

She was fully formed.

A woman with life, and humour and

Hopes.

And in the gaps between the dark times,

She talked about her dreams,

And all the reasons they never happened.

But by then, we had a fight on our hands,

For she was slowly leaking back

Bit by bit, thought by thought,

To where she came from.

For the stars wanted her back,

And there was nothing we could do.

WORDS TO FIT A TWEET

Be happy, pal don't just smile for others

The years are eaten up that way

And the emptiness will lie beyond

When those you smile to

Go away.

BE KIND

The night of him looking at the stars was the night
that everything changed.

That night as the planets danced overhead, a
thought grabbed him and shot right up his nose
and into his brain, almost taking his breath away.

Here he was abandoned in Space, a traveller and
whatever the dimensions of this Universe, there
could only be so many travellers.

Whatever brought him or sent him to this place –
and whatever he was going through was unique –
perhaps what he was experiencing really meant
something. There was a reason for his being

If that was true, then everyone else he knew or
met or saw was travelling too – all of them wound
up by a key and sent on a path with little decision
on their part of what they should take.

If they had all been moulded by a god – the woman
in the bakery, or the postman, or the kid who
always cried, then they had an angel at their birth –
but even if their heart, their existence or their
imagination was an accident of the Universe – they
were still unique, still special, still a traveller.

So, whether he jumped to conclusions or jumped to attention or jumped out of the way, he told himself to remember – no one asked to be a traveller.
Be kind.

THE HISTORY OF A KISS

The last time I was home, I gave my mother a kiss,
And somewhere, sometime long ago, she kissed my
great-grandmother,
Who kissed her brother just before he set off to
fight in World War one,
And although he died a few days before the end of
the war,
He had kissed a young French girl in a bar, and they
said that they would meet someday after the
troubles,
And the French girl kissed her father and told him
of the Scotsman whom she liked,
And years before her father had kissed the girl's
mother in a little hotel in London,
And that night they had gone to see Charles
Dickens as he read from Great Expectations,
And the girl's mother kissed Dickens and said thank
you for the story,
And told him that her boyfriend had just asked her
to be his wife,
And after that night's reading, Dickens gave his
daughter a goodnight kiss,
And his daughter kissed her pillow and dreamed of
her one true love.

SUNRISE ON STRAWBERRY HILL

I come up here when someone is born, or a person has left, or a heart has gone.

For all sorts of reasons, I walk this hill. As I get older, I realise that you bring more ghosts up here with you each time you climb.

That is what ageing is all about – collecting ghosts.

I think of the arguments with those long departed, and I realise each and every one of us gets it wrong – yet we all do it in the most spectacular ways.

I understand that I learn more on a dark day than I do on a sunny. So here we are – another morning, another sunrise, another chance to put something right.

However small.

And as I walk back down, I can feel a little hope in my soul for the day ahead.
That is what life is all about – getting it wrong and trying to fix it.

CHARLIE TURNER, ONCE IN A BLUE MOON

Strange things happen to nice people.

There I've said it, but it doesn't make it any less true, friends. I ain't gonna argue here, and now about how you measure niceness and all, you're just gonna have to take my hand-on-my-heart word on that point. You see, me and my pals, sure are the nicest people to walk this part of Bucks County – may be even further, but heck, if it just doesn't stop things happening.

I guess the first kookiest thing to happen was when my grandmother lost that precious ring, the one that my grandpappy had given to her on the day she said yes to marrying him. Charlie (that's my best friend) just turned to her and said, you'll find it under that old leather chair your cat uses as a bed. And you know what? That was where it was. Well, I'll be, I kept saying to myself that day, well if that ain't the darndest thing.

My first thought was that Charlie had put it there himself, on account, he was always up to something or other. But then, as Charlie said himself, he'd never been up to that part of my grandmother's house that held the cat's chair. I don't think he was lying, friends. I surely don't. I guess Charlie had always been the weird one –

well, weirder than the rest of us – which is a long way away from what folks call normal in these parts.

Charlie used to go by the name of 'Kenzo, The Magician' when he was knee-high to a real magician. He used to put on shows for us kids, even convinced us that he could make birds appear out of the air. Then one day, Danny, Charlie's young cousin from his pa's family, bust a finger when a brick fell on it. That finger couldn't make up its mind which way it was pointing. Then Charlie took his cousin's hand and placed it between his own hands. Danny said he felt really warm, and when Charlie took his hands away, the finger was pointing the way it was meant to. I kid you not, friends. It was pointing as straight as the day is long.

Somewhere, at the back of my mind, I think the two of them had conjured this up between them ('scuse my words), but that night, Charlie swore on my life that he didn't do nothing sneaky. The look in my pal's eyes made me know he wasn't lying.

One day, not long after my birthday, I was playing in the yard with the hamster that my folks had given me. I can't really remember what happened, but my mom called out to me for something, and I turned to ask her what she wanted when Geronimo (the hamster) kinda made an escape right into the middle of the street. It was just as Mister Feeling's horseless carriage was put-put-putting along (with Mister Feeling singing a loud song from Don Giovanni) that he ran over my hamster.

I think it was my screaming that brought Charlie running – I must have been loud to hear it over Mister Feeling.

"What's happened, little brother?" That's what Charlie always called me, on account that I was shorter than him.

"He's killed Geronimo,' I screamed.

Charlie went over to the flattened hamster and picked him up.

"No, he ain't, lookie here, little brother."

Sure enough, Geronimo was running up and down Charlie's arm and nibbling his ear like he was at the peak of his life.

"I musta been mistaken," I said to my pal.

"No, you weren't," said Charlie, and he wandered off whistling to himself.

These strange things kept happening – but far enough apart that no one ever really joined the dots. I guess when folks would talk about Charlie behind his back, I would get really annoyed and punch anyone who said my bestest pal was weird. He ain't weird, I told them. My mom told me that folks like Charlie only come along once in a blue moon.

When we'd finished schooling forever, I went off to learn how to be an artist, and Charlie joined the army as a doctor or something. Apart from a postcard here and there, we kinda lost touch.

Then one day, not long after my Pa started talking strange like, talking about things and people who weren't there, Charlie turned up at the door.

"I've come to fix things," he said and walked straight into the house without a hello or anything.

"Where's Henry?" That was my Pa's name.

"He's sick," I said.

"I know he's sick. I've come to help him."

I told Charlie that my Pa was in the back bedroom and that Charlie wasn't to be alarmed. You see, my Pa kinda liked to be by himself and be with the folks he said were in the room. I couldn't even see any of them.

"Just 'cause he sees them, don't mean they're there. And just 'cause you can't, don't mean they aren't," then Charlie started his whistling again as if he knew something I didn't. That wouldn't have been difficult.

"We are such things as memories; that is all we are," exclaimed Charlie. I asked him if Shakespeare had said that, and he said it was, then continued whistling.

I remember my grandpappy had said that Charlie was an 'enigma', which I thought was a monster like a vampire or something. But when I looked it up in the book of words, it said that Charlie was the kinda friend that no one could work out. Those were the kinda friends that I liked.

When Charlie came back down from my Pa's room, he just said that everything was fixed, that he'd meet me tomorrow on Main Street at three.

"Don't be late."

As Charlie closed the front door behind him, my father was standing at the kitchen door, scratching himself.

"I could eat a horse," that was what he said, and he whistled the same tune that Charlie whistled, then my Pa went in and cooked the biggest steak in the world. My Pa never talked of people I couldn't see again.

Charlie never got really famous for anything, but folks eventually talked about him in friendly terms. Whenever someone had an illness or a doctor gave them little time to live, people would call on Charlie, and sometimes things would get better and sometimes they wouldn't.

"I guess the universe ain't taking 'no' for an answer this time," he'd say.

On the day that Charlie died, the whole town showed up. I was picked to say a few things about my pal, the enigma, but first I got the whole congregation to whistle Charlie's tune (he would have liked that), even the reverend had to smile. On his gravestone, I had them carve the words:

'CHARLIE TURNER – ONCE, IN A BLUE MOON'.

I reckon he would have liked that, too.

PAINTED LOVE

When the flowers had all but disappeared from
Clare's garden, she had replaced them by painting
roses and daffodils on a brick wall at the rear of her
flower bed. There would be no beautiful smells
welcoming a visitor as they walked up her path, but
then there hadn't been any visitors in such a long
time – at least not since that peculiar day.

Last Spring, when her car had finally given up the
ghost, she had painted a newer, flashier model on
the garage door. She stood back and smiled at
what looked like the best car she had ever owned.

Sometime in November, Clare painted the
downstairs' room all in white and then, one by one,
she painted each of her family members on the
walls around the room. When it was finished, and
she had pushed the table against the back of the
room, it looked as if her family would be there with
her for Christmas, all sitting at the one big table.
She smiled because nothing like that had ever
really happened in those days long ago. She had
even painted in her grandparents and those long-
remembered pals who had left this life too soon.

Clare placed plates in front of each painted figure,
and somewhere in the attic, she found an old wind-
up gramophone. There was one record – a big
heavy shellac disc with a song titled 'I Don't Want

to Set the World on Fire', and given the circumstances, she had to laugh at the irony. It was meant to be played at 78 RPM, but Clare sometimes over-wound it so that it played too fast and then too slow. It made Clare smile, and she sang along with it, again and again, regardless of the speed.

She painted turkey and peas and potatoes on the plates, and for her Aunty Sue (who was a vegetarian), she had painted a selection of vegetables.

Clare had conversations with all of them at the meal – not that things like that had really happened in life. At her old Christmas' meals, everyone spoke at the same time. But hey, that was what living was about, and that was what people were about. She missed them all.

Before Clare knew it, she was throwing a New Year's Party. She asked each of her painted family to make a resolution. Then she made one herself; hers was simple: to find a partner and settle down. Clare was sure she heard all her friends and family applaud.

'At last,', she could hear them saying. 'About time,' was another.

She painted out a few ideas for partners, but most of them were based on old boyfriends, and all of them entirely wrong for her. Then one cold night, she found a bottle of brandy in the cellar – it must have been there years. She'd promised herself that she would only have one sip every birthday, but in the end, greed and loneliness got the better of her, and she drank most of the bottle.

When she awoke the next afternoon, she found that she had painted a partner on the canvas – one that she would have never gone out with in the old times. He was more exciting somehow. He was new and, more than that, an undiscovered land.

She wasn't sure if it was the hangover, but she could have sworn on a Bible that he had winked at her. Later, when she was having her usual daily cry at the window, she heard someone calling her name – of course, she knew that was impossible, for as far she was concerned, there wasn't anyone left. She was the last woman and probably the last human on the planet.

"Clare," there it was again.

She turned to see her partner, her boyfriend, her lover lift himself from the painting and beckon her to come to him.

Clare stopped, and a cold chill filled her blood. She realised that she had probably finally gone insane. All those years, all that time being alone – all that poor mental health. Then she lifted up her spirits, and she smiled to herself, realising that it didn't really matter that much – not now – and kissed her lover.

What a way to go, she thought, what a bloody brilliant way to go.

CHARLIE'S DAD AND THE YELLOW BALLOON

His name was Charlie, and he was a kid. Charlie was lucky enough to be living through his best years. His mother, father, brother, and sisters were all healthy, all happy, and all in that perfect little bubble that happens from time to time in life.

When Charlie was eight, he had his first birthday party, which involved all his friends coming to his house. This was Charlie's first proper party.

Charlie's parents were like ducks on the water, everything seemed calm on top, but both of them had to paddle extremely hard to keep themselves and the family from sinking. Not that Charlie knew any of this or the double shifts that his father had worked that previous week to afford Charlie's first grown-up party.

Charlie, his brother, and his Dad all blew up the balloons. Charlie inflated the red ones, his brother the green balloons and his Dad the yellow ones. Both Charlie and his brother used little air pumps to inflate them all, but Charlie's Dad just blew them up with his own breath. This was his youngest son's first real party, and he wanted to give it everything he had.

That night, after the party, Charlie's Dad felt a pain in his left arm, then his chest, and with only time to quietly say 'goodbye', he closed his eyes for good.

The following day, Charlie's grandfather took down all the decorations – anything that reminded the family of happier times – and burst all the balloons. Or so he thought.

Charlie sat in his bedroom, scared to cry for his Dad since he felt that if he started again, he would never stop. That was when he noticed the yellow balloon in the corner of the room, with a little note attached 'Happy Birthday, my boy, I am so proud of you, love dad'.

Suddenly it struck Charlie that there was still a part of his Dad alive. In the balloon was his Dad's breath – a little piece of him – something that he had made while he was happy.

So, Charlie very carefully drew a little face on the yellow balloon and talked to it as if it were his Dad. In the corner of his room was a little bit of his father, and he was still with him. When Charlie woke in the morning, the balloon was still watching over him.

The next night he could hear his mother crying in her room, and so Charlie took the balloon into her room and told her the story. That night the two of them slept in her bed, watched over by the balloon filled with his Dad's breath.

Charlie tried everything he could to stop the balloon from getting smaller and smaller – his Dad was disappearing and leaving Charlie for good. Charlie's grandfather heard his grandson crying and came into the room to help. Charlie told his grandfather about the balloon and how it was losing his Dad's air.

His grandfather held Charlie and told him that it was only his Dad returning home. His grandfather, and Charlie, and Charlie's Dad didn't come from here – they came from out there – far away in Space. He told him that Charlie's Dad would need his breath out in the stars and that it had to return to him. Charlie's grandfather said that Charlie could keep the balloon with him to remember his Dad, but in the end, it was what a person left in your heart that counted – nothing else.

DOBBIN'S LITTLE RAILWAY STATION

There is a little railway station just north of somewhere and to the east of that other place. And one time in your life, you'll either have stood waiting on a train there or will have passed through it, I promise you.

The station wasn't anything special; it just helped people get into the city and received their tired bodies at the end of the day.

It had been built in the 1850s and judging by the architecture. It was a statement to a country with an empire. But things change, and empires fall, and now the station just had a ticket office and a toilet.

It wasn't small enough that people talked to each other, nor was it big enough to get lost in – it was a station of an awkward size, where people saw the same folks every day but were standing too far away to communicate. And life went on, as it does.

Then one cold November, just after that thing that happened, but just before that other thing was about to occur, Dobbin came to the station as the Station Manager.

Okay, all he did was sell tickets and clean the toilet, but that wasn't going to stop Dobbin – who had once dreamt he would be an astronaut or, failing that, regenerate into Doctor Who.

At first, Dobbin (who had never been actually told to his face that life was hard) started singing as he sold the tickets. There were those (as there are always 'those') who found the humming and singing a distraction, but for most, it was a little break from the hum-drum of travelling to work.

Then Dobbin started to sing as he announced what trains were going to which destinations and the ones which weren't coming. A few faces would crack a smile while standing on the platform, and possibly, one or two would forget about their troubles for a few minutes.

It wasn't long before Dobbin was telling little stories for the folks who stood, waiting. About how he had got the job, how he had never been picked for sports teams at school and how, despite everything, he felt that a Station Manager was a brilliant job, and he wanted to thank everyone who had helped him.

One or two of those waiting broke into applause, and like an Oscar speech, Dobbin decided to thank everyone in his life.

One morning, a note was left at the ticket office, which just said 'thank you', and Dobbin felt that

that was the best note he had ever been given in his life.

In between the songs, the selling of the tickets, the cleaning of the toilet, and the little speeches, Dobbin started to write his own little stories.

One snowy day when everyone was generally feeling miserable, he made this announcement:

"Good day, my fellow travellers. I want you to think about your problems. I guess most of you are standing there thinking of them anyway. Now, in your head, give your problems away to someone in the station, and you take their problems. Swap yours for theirs. And I know you've probably heard it before but I, reckon that if you could actually see all their problems, you'd be screaming for your own back."

Then Dobbin broke into his version of Bohemian Rhapsody (doing all the voices). The station became so popular that people started to change stations and leave from Dobbin's because it made their day. It got so crowded that sometimes there wasn't room to move.

The big chiefs on the Railway Board decided to investigate and discovered that Dobbin's spirit and outlook were just what they needed at one of the big city stations.

Soon he started to run the Dobbin's School for Railway Enhancement and Entertainment. Dobbin realised that all people really wanted was someone to tell them that they were okay.

Dobbin is the Prime Minister now and, of course, broadcasts a song to the entire country every morning. Today the song was the Beatles' 'Here Comes the Sun', and folks in every city, town and hamlet were heard to sing along with him.

HAVE A WONDERFUL DAY

It's today, and no matter how hard you fought it, you woke up,

Some people won't and wanted to, just to put things right,

You can read, just as you're doing now,

Some people can't and would love to with all their hearts,

You can work a computer, a pad, a phone,

Some people have never seen one,

One day soon, you might be on your way somewhere,

Many people will have nowhere to go,

It might be today, and even 'though you may not think so,

You are already blessed in many ways.

Have a great, great day.

THE SONGBIRD

Some hearts are born to do specific tasks, and so it was with the songbird. She had been brought into the Universe to sing her song so that others could hear and benefit.

Not that the songbird ever noticed, for each morning she would fly to the top of the highest tree and sing her heart out – that was the way she had been made, and so it was the most natural thing for her to do.

One cold winter's day, an old woman happened to pass the tree when she was on her way back from the cemetery where she had placed flowers on her husband's grave. As we all get tired, she was tired, so she sat below the highest tree for a rest. She closed her eyes and wished that they would stay closed forever so that she could meet again with her love, but then it happened – she heard the songbird, and the sweet music warmed her heart to the world once more. The old woman raised herself from her rest and decided she would try another day, for one never knew what was around the next corner.

The snows soon melted, and the winter became the Spring, and still, the songbird sang her tunes.

One afternoon as the flowers were coming to life, a fearful lad from the next village was on his way to meet his love. He stopped below the tree to think about the love of his life and of all the things he wanted to say but was afraid.

Then the songbird sang her song, and the lad realised that this was a world of one-time chances and that if he didn't tell his love now, he might never get another. He skipped to his love's house whistling the tune of the songbird and spilled his heart out.

A child from several mountains over was struck with an illness, and the only doctor who could help the poor child lived over the tops of several mountains the other way. So, her father carried the child over the mountain, down the valley and over the next mountain until he was so crippled in pain he could not go on. By chance, he happened to sit beneath the highest tree just as the songbird started to sing, and as he rested, he realised if there was that much beauty in the world, then he could carry his sick child the rest of the way to the doctor.

And so, the songbird sang and sang and helped each and every one who passed the tree.

The following year when the warm winds came to the hills, the songbird gave birth to her own little songbird. She had waited all her life for such an event. She would fly into the forest and bring back food, singing her tunes, and she knew that one day, her own little songbird would sing a tune of their own.

One day when the songbird was out looking for food, a wind came and blew so hard that the little nest and her baby were blown down from the highest tree.

When the songbird returned to her tree, she saw her little one lying on the forest floor, eyes closed and no longer breathing.

That was when it happened; the songbird lost her song. She could no longer sing. There was nothing wrong with her, just that her heart no longer wanted to – and so the forest became quiet.

When the old woman heard of the troubles of the songbird and how she had lost her song, she decided to visit the little bird. She sat with the songbird and caressed her and thanked her for all her songs.

Then a strange thing happened, the songbird let out one note – one pure and beautiful note. The old woman told the lad who was once fearful, and he too visited the songbird and thanked her for her tunes, and suddenly the songbird sang another, different beautiful note.

And so it was that all the people who the songbird had helped came to visit, and each brought a musical note back to the songbird.

And although it took some time, and perhaps the tunes were not as heartfelt as they once were, the songbird was able to sing again, and the Universe smiled.

WORDS

Words can misfire, be misplaced or misused
Words can slice through a heart with hate or with
love
Words can shrivel a hope
Words can laugh, words can dance or sing
Words can destroy everything you are or ever will
be
Words can fill an empty life with visions of another
Words can build walls or break them down
Words can pin your head to the pillow
Words can lift your eyes to the heavens
Words are beautiful, and words are dangerous
Words can condemn, and words can save
Words can cause you to fall, and words can send
you soaring
Words come from you, and words come from me
Whatever your words, whenever your words
Use them wisely.

TONIGHT

Tonight, I saw a solar storm,

Which brought the heavens to its knees,

And seared the eyes and hearts of those who watched.

I tasted nectar and ambrosia.

And sat with kings and gods,

And talked of words with Shakespeare.

Tonight, I flew with Orville Wright,

And gasped,

As air beneath us passed.

Then ran across the Milky Way,

And shouted at the stars.

Tonight, I fought my enemy,

At the battle of the Somme,

And wept where comrades fell

Somewhere beyond the poppy fields.

Tonight, I sat with Einstein,

And over tea,

We talked of Time and Space,

Then he smiled and laughed with me.

Tonight, I tasted life and cried

And swept the Universe entire,

Which sat inside my head

And you ask me why I write.

I AM ENOUGH

When the withering sunshine slowly starts to rust

And my darker days are quietly growing tough

I close my eyes and smile somewhere inside,

And tell myself a dozen times:

"I am enough".

BREATHLESS

.... if she had looked up at that moment, his nurse would have seen his toes moving in waltz time to a tune that only he could hear. Through the willow window, he could see the stars and the Moon, and he remembered how, as a child, he would lie on his back and be overwhelmed by the wonder at it all. But now he was old and almost finished, yet he still could conjure a picture in his head of him at seventeen dancing to the Blue Danube. And that was his final thought before life finally took him back. If there was a God, and he felt sure that there was, then the music was some part of God - a sliver that rippled across the Universe, an echo of God's love, and to the man, this was greater than all the wonders of the World. But if there was no god, then the waltz was written by an ape that had only recently walked upright and had created these notes while it cried to the stars: and that, to him, was just as breath-taking.....

MEET YOU ON THE DARK SIDE OF THE MOON

My Granddad is on the far side of the Moon.

Well, he used to call it the Dark Side, after his favourite record that he would never stop playing, but later he found out that it wasn't dark and that it just pointed away from us all the time.

"That's the kind of place I'd like to go for a holiday," he would say to me, then kiss the top of my head. "Nice and quiet, and if I wanted to look at my old home, I just need to pop round to the near side, and there the Earth would be. You could give me a wave," he said, then he would spit on his handkerchief and wipe the chocolate from my face. I never did like the hanky.

When he would take me outside to look up at the Moon, he always said: "In the name of the wee man," although I wasn't sure who the 'wee man' was.

Sometimes, if it were a bright full moon, he would shout out, "Jesus, would you look at that, isn't it just the bee's knees?" Yep, I was none the wiser about that too, but I think he was either telling Jesus or shouting to him because I think Jesus might live on the Moon.

When I was eight years old, they put my Granddad in a rocket ship, a wooden one that sat on a table in a hall. But they didn't launch him into Space (as I had hoped); instead, they slid him in behind some curtains, and we all sang songs. I guess that's the way he would want his rocket launch to be like. As everyone sang about this and that and Granddad's pal, Jesus, I counted down, 10...9...8.... the curtains closed just as I got to 'lift-off', and I knew then he was gone.

Some nights I look out the window of my room, and I say, "In the name of the wee man, would you look at that."

I know he can hear me, and I know he sometimes pops around to the sunny side to wave.
I miss you, Granddad.

FOOTPRINTS ON A CARPET

Even if it's only footprints on a carpet

Or blades of grass crushed where I once sat

Or a muddy scar upon a garage wall

Where my hand had leaned upon

Or a thumbprint on a pane of glass

On that day, we talked and talked

Or a smile that made your face light up

When you thought of what I said

Or a note left out to tell you news

Now crushed and thrown away

Or a space that I once stood upon

Now emptier in the absence

Even for just one of those

That I am remembered by – then I'll be satisfied,

I was here.

WALKING EACH OTHER HOME

Whether you're tired,

Or feeling alone,

Each of us walks

The other, home.

It's brief this life

Much on our own

But we're all just walking,

Each other, home.

THE BALLAD OF THE QUIET MAN

He said nothing, not a word ever passed his lips; He just sat in the peace and quiet with a Mona Lisa smile.

One cold day the Angry People passed his way. They all shouted about this, that and the other. Then they stopped and asked the quiet man if he was angry.

He said not a word, and the Angry People liked that, "This man is so angry about this and that and the other, he is seething with rage". They shook his hand, and on they went.

Then one summer's evening, the sad folks were passing by, and they looked at the quiet man and then sat beside him, "This man is mourning; this man says nothing, but the sadness shows upon his face". They wept beside the quiet man then walked on down the road.

On an afternoon like any other, a stupid man was walking through as he was lost. He asked the quiet man the way to town, and when he didn't reply, the stupid man smiled and said, "I see you are as stupid as I am. 'Tis better to say nothing and not look the fool". The stupid man wished his stupid brother well and continued to be lost.

Just before the start of autumn, some happy people were running and jumping and came to rest next to the quiet man, "Look here," one shouted, "This man is so happy that he smiles in his contentment". And the people all cheered and carried him shoulder-high down the lane towards the town.

This happened to the quiet man more than he would have liked, and once again, he had to walk all the way back home.

SHOREHAM AND THE GEESE

Most of her 94 years had been spent in this beautiful little corner of the world. The rear of her property looked up to the Cross on the hill above, and now that most of her days were spent resting in bed – she found this a favourable view. In the Spring and the Summer months, she watched the little birds and then the wild geese as they came to visit in her back yard and the fields beyond.

It hadn't always been this way. In her younger, vibrant days, she worked on the farm and later in the Cooperative shop on the village High Street.

She had been born into a place that had meant the most happiness and, therefore, had never wanted to leave. She had been married for a short time, there had been no children, but she had accepted that fact and moved on with her life. Her husband had always wanted sons and daughters and had eventually found a family with his second wife in Hastings.

In all her 94 years, much of it had been spent looking from her window on to the passers-by and their changing tastes and fashions – and as the older residents had aged and passed on, so the village constantly invigorated itself with newer, younger dynamic families. Most of these folks now worked in the city and spent much of their time commuting. She had been lucky. She had found everything she needed within reach. Not many had had that chance.

But the main thing that preoccupied her thoughts was the magic in this little haven. Her great Grandmother, a woman who had been there at the opening of the Co-op shop – in the same year that Queen Victoria had died – had always told her the same sentence over and over again, 'Shoreham finds you, you don't find Shoreham'.

She had always wondered what that had meant – but it wasn't about the likes of herself or her family. It was about the souls who thought they had discovered this hamlet by accident – a lucky accident – but an accident all the same.

Yet she knew the truth. They came here incomplete, or sad, or single, or unhappily married, or sick, or healthy, or hopeful, or lost – and they stayed long enough to put things right in their lives. To find that special person, or to lose the wrong one. To beat the depression or some disease or another.

To raise a family or find a new one. To see the end of loneliness in the company of new friends or to find confidence when it was lacking.

Whatever their needs, Shoreham grabbed them as they passed by, then dusted them down and didn't let go until the time was right for them to move on.

She had seen it time and time again – enough to know that it wasn't a fluke but a certainty – a miracle.

It was a truth that not everyone came to the village searching for something, but most did. They just didn't know it. And from her little window on the High Street, she had watched them find it and had taken comfort in their happiness and their newfound lives.

Now from her bedroom window, she watched as the geese came to the field beyond the trees.

Those beautiful birds waited on her to close her eyes for the very last time, and then they carried her soul to that far country where she could rest.

I STILL LOVE YOU

I

Still love you

Though

It's been a

Long time, it's been a

Lifetime of

Living without you.

Our secret moments scar the

Visions I have of anyone

Else.

You were everything – a

Once chance meeting in this lonely

Universe.

HOW COULD YOU BE ANYTHING OTHER THAN
BEAUTIFUL?

So, you're not as thin, nor as fat, as you wanted to
be,
Or as tall, or as short, or with a little more hair,
You're not as clever or wise as they said that you
were,
Or have looks that have people chasing you there.

And you're not that great person with so many
friends,
Or as famous or rich as you dreamed life would
bring,
But the dust of the stars was moulded and shaped
Into the soul that is you,
By someone
Or something.

You're not as graceful or talented as you hoped you
would be,
Or have a family and home that was always packed
full,
But you're loved and unique, and somebody cares,

How could you be anything other than beautiful?

THE DAY I HEARD THE NEWS

The day I heard the news,

The world didn't end – at least not that day.

Instead, the sky grew a little darker,

And I realised there was no longer any way

That we'd accidentally bump into one another

On some far-flung shore and laugh about the old times.

That morning I said, 'see you later' was to be our very last and

Neither of us even knew.

The day I heard the news,

A billion candles on the Sun blew themselves out,

And my shadow grew a little paler against the Earth.

WHAT ARE YOU SAVING YOURSELF FOR?

You hesitate to say hello –
To that girl or boy,
To the stranger needing help,
You think twice about some invitation -
Another day, another time perhaps.

You aren't ready, least not today
What with this and that, you have to do.
And so that chance you should have taken,
Has flown, has gone, has disappeared.

What are you saving your little self for?
Are you so sure of another chance?
Another day, another tune,
So certain of that one more dance?

What are you saving your little heart for?
Some far off day when your luck will flow?
Why delay and wait on something,
When the end is closer than you know.

YOU AND ME

Let you and me

Lie quietly

Touching side by side

To watch the rust sun setting

As the day grows dark outside

We've travelled half the Universe

We're formed from stars and dust

The miracle is –

We found each other

In love,

And hope,

And trust.

THE GIRL WHO STOLE A PIECE OF THE SUN

I think I was eight or nine years of age when my Grandma went down the road. At least that's what my Granddad called it.

"Your Grandma has gone down the road, and I'm afraid she won't be back," he said with sad eyes.

"What never?"

"Listen, sweet-pea, one day I'll take that walk and later, so will you. We'll all meet up at the little shack further down the road, just over the first hill. You remember that I'll see you there."

My name is Sara, by the way, and I always remembered that story from my Granddad. On that day, the day that my Grandma took the walk, my Granddad took me into the city to show me how to be happy in times when the World goes a little dark.

"Anytime you want to talk to your Grandma, just say 'hey Grandma' and then tell her how you feel."

"She'll hear me?"

"Of course, she will, saying 'hey Grandma' is like pushing buttons on your telephone," said Granddad with a big, huge grin.

"And I'll show you another thing to show she's listening."

And my Granddad led me into a railway station nearby.

"Whenever you feel lonely," he said. "Or sad, just stand on this spot and say to your Grandma 'please make people look at me, Grandma'".

And do you know what? People were staring at us, and I said 'thank you, Grandma' to myself.

It was only years later I realised we were standing in front of the railway departures board, but still, it worked, and I couldn't help smiling.

Then my Granddad took me to the park and to the little pond where they sailed model boats.

It was just then that the Sun came out, and from his little bag, my Granddad took out an old glass jar, one with a lid.

"Look sweet-pea," and my Granddad pointed to the Sun's reflection in the water. "See the sun?"

"I do, Granddad, I do."

And then he put the glass jar in the pond and filled it with water. And just then, the Sun disappeared, and my Granddad told me he had caught a piece of the Sun in a jar. Then he put the lid on it.

"I want you to put this jar under your bed, sweet-pea, and when you feel dark, or you miss your Grandma, just open the jar and let some of the sun fill up your room."

My Granddad took his walk a few years ago, but you know what? I've still got that jar with me, the one where we captured a little piece of the Sun. And on dark days, I still open the lid.

LEAVING TRACES

Don't think you are never seen, dear friend,

You leave a trace wherever you wander –

A smile, a laugh, a hope.

Don't think you are never heard, my pal

There is always someone listening –

A song, a word, a joke.

Don't think you are ever forgotten, old friend,

For when we passed each other

In that briefest of time,

You left a piece of you with me

That I'll carry wherever I go.

THE HOUSE BESIDE THE SEA

There was love above and below me in that house that stood beside the sea.

On clear days I could spot the horizon, and that meant everything to me. It was the tallest of houses and the happiest of homes. It was stuffed full to the rafters with sisters and brothers and my mother and father.

We helped each other, and we supported one another. We made each other smile, and sometimes we made each other cry. These were the days that were warmed by the Sun and seemed to last forever.

In the winter, we drank broth and ate stews and hunkered down in the heat of each other's company, comfortable that the others were there. There were card games, singing, communal cooking and laughter, oh yes, the laughter. There was always someone laughing in that house. When the storms hit the house, it rocked and swayed and the more it rocked and swayed, the more we felt safe. Don't ask me what I mean by that, just that you had to be there to understand.

My Grandpa had built it for the simple reason that he wanted to prove you could build a house on the sand by the sea. There were those in town who said he was a brick short of a chimney, but my

Grandpa had always believed in himself, and so it had happened. And having been built by such a kind soul and even kinder heart meant that the very building seemed to bleed understanding and tolerance.

When it swayed in the wind, it sang to us. The building felt as if it was telling you that nothing was going to harm you. We were just to relax and bend with the wind. There was a writing room, or rather I used it to write in it, but my brothers and sisters would read, paint, listen to the radio, have heartfelt discussions about the world and all the stars in it. I learned many things about life in that room and some things I probably shouldn't have.

I realise now how lucky I was back then, what with all that softness, that gentleness, that amount of caring from my family; all of it given to me by some higher force. Boy, was I the lucky one? My father and mother taught us never ever to take anything for granted. To smell the rain, to feel the flowers, to stand on the roof of the house some days and just scream, scream for your very existence.

Sometimes I'd scream for the overwhelming energy that was the world, and sometimes I would scream for all the injustices that we heap on each other (even on ourselves), for there is no crueller person in the world than those things we do to our own minds and hearts. It's like the man said, if we treated other people the way we treated ourselves, we wouldn't last long.

So I wrote and wrote about the way things changed and the way that things stayed the same. I wrote about love and hate and war and peace. Those days were the most perfect of my life. But as I've written in these pages before, no one ever tells you that you are passing perfection – you only ever see it in the rearview mirror, and that's when you realise that there's no reverse.

Each morning I could smell the cinnamon wafting its way up the stairs to my room, and a few seconds later, it was helped along by the smell of the coffee. My mother would be standing at the back porch with the wind coming in off the sea, both hands around her cup of hot brew and deeply breathing in the air.

"Good morning, my much-loved and cherished son," she'd say.
I forgot to mention that my mother came with a warning: she was a crazy as a box of frogs.
"And how has the universe treated you this fine morning?" she'd ask.
"Fine." I'd say – I was trying real hard to cultivate a mysterious air about me at the time, given the fact that I intended to be a writer.

"You don't say," then she'd smile, pull her housecoat in tight and head back to making the

biscuits for breakfast.
Sometimes I would sit with a hand under my chin,
waiting on the rest of the family to come down,
trying to look European (although I wasn't real sure
what that meant). Other times I would sit with
Grandpa's old pipe and stare out to sea as if the
meaning of life were somewhere out there to be
found. Man, that pipe tasted real bad.

I went through a spell of chewing tobacco, but it
was short-lived due to the vomiting. Then I got a
big hat, and I decided that was the look for me.

There was a real hot summer when I would wear
the hat from first thing in the morning to last thing
at night. I even slept with the hat on, but I guess
someone would take it off my head when I was fast
asleep – while I was dreaming of the future life that
I was going to live in that hat.

To be a writer in the last house on the beach was
indeed the best thing ever in the world.

One morning, my father came to breakfast and told
everyone to remain calm and not worry, but
Grandma had been taken to the hospital. She had
been my Moon and my stars when I was growing
up. She was the one who encouraged me to write,
who had read Dickens to me and who now would
listen to my own stories.

She'd never say if a story was good or bad, but

when she said, "My ain't that interesting", I knew then it wasn't one of her favourites.

She and my Grandpa lived in the best room at the top of the house, the one with the views and the sunshine, although it always seemed to be full of sunshine when my Grandma was there.

In the evening, when I was writing, I could hear the dance music coming from their gramophone. Boy, they loved to dance. When they were younger, they would travel the county taking part in competitions. Their room was packed to the roof with trophies.

When my Grandpa started to get sick, neither of them talked about the illness until the moment that my Grandpa said that perhaps they shouldn't dance any more. The day that my Grandma got sick, I went to the hospital in the afternoon, and she was sitting up in bed and smiling. Boy, that made me feel a whole lot better.

Every day after school, I went straight to the hospital and read her my latest story. At the weekends, if she felt okay, she would read me some of David Copperfield.

In her final week, she asked to be allowed home; I didn't know that she was finished. I honestly thought she was getting better. About two days before she left us for good, and while the nurse was downstairs getting a coffee, she asked me to take her to the roof and bring the wind-up gramophone.

When we got up there, boy, it was warm, and you could see for miles. I turned the handle on the gramophone and put on her favourite tune, and then she asked me to dance. I took her hand, and I bowed, and then we danced as if she was seventeen again.

FAULT LINES

It will never be perfect,
My Grandmother said,
Not your life, not your love,
Not your heart or your head,
It will never be perfect,
And you can't make it so,
Just accept there are fault lines,
And let the rest go.

HOPE

H old
O n,
P ain
E nds

H ave
O nly
P ositive
E xpectations

H appiness
O utlives
P eople's
E rrors

H ope
O neday,
P repare
E veryday

H old
O n,
P roblems
E nd

Always. x

COMING HOME

When he stepped from the train, there was still heat in the air. He could smell the fields and the soil, and as he looked across the platform, he was sure he could see his father walking up to the station to meet him. But like everything else in his life, they were all gone a long time ago.

He'd been back for his father's death, of course, and he had thought about all the things they would say to each other in the final hours – but his father had slipped away with only a smile and soft squeeze of his son's hand.

He lifted his rucksack over his shoulder and headed down the stairs to Station Road. Things were still very much the same. The road was a little newer, and the hedges looked a little different from what he remembered, but it was still home. In the field, he could imagine his mother waving back from all those years ago. Smiling and alive, not touched by the bad ending.

He could see the light in the window of the Rectory. There would be a new vicar living there now – one he didn't know. He had lived through three vicars, and all of them had helped him at difficult times in his life. Whatever was said, the village needed a church and a vicar. It was somewhere to be thought of as special.

As he turned the corner, he held his breath. There was the Old George – with maybe a little more painted makeup, a little more front but still the same old place. He and his pals had drunk there, perhaps a little earlier than the law would have allowed, but that was life in a small village. There had been a family who had owned it for as long as he could remember. It was easy to forget, as a child running in and out of the place, that it was someone's home as well as a bar.

A couple of walkers were sitting enjoying an ale as he passed by, so he stopped and watched. The Old George had been inviting folks to sit and rest for a long, long time now; the farmers, the bikers, the musicians, the Morris dancers, all had sat and supped; all had talked about their lives and loves, all had discussed their troubles – all were gone now.

The church gate was still as he had remembered that day when it had been decked with flowers for his sister's wedding. Her body lay in the churchyard now – it had done for some seventeen years.

He turned past Church Cottages and into Church Street – he was sure he remembered a shop in that street, but his memory came and went these days. It was hard to be sure of what had been and what was the tainted memories of an old man.

As he walked down the street, he could see the dying Sun reflecting on the river, and it made him feel the way it always had. It made him feel warm inside, just like a good whisky. He had sat by the river, man and boy, and it had been the one constant in his life.

Two children were trying to catch fish from the bridge, just like he had done back then, and like him, the kids were pulling up empty hooks. But it was the comradeship, the feeling of safety, the feeling of a village watching over you while you fished that had kept him happy as a child. Nowhere else in the world had he ever felt as safe and happy as he had on those days as a boy sitting on the bridge – fishing.

The Sun had seemed warmer and brighter back then. Probably another trick of his old mind. He turned to look back at where the Rising Sun pub had been. Some nights he would sit by the river waiting on his father to come out of the 'Sun and bring him a lemonade.

"Cheers, dad," he'd say, and his Dad would ruffle his hair. Just to do that once again, he thought – just once.

Folks were eating outside the King's Arms – a new generation of people from London and all the areas in between, having a day in the country. That was the village's lifeblood – visitors, it kept the pubs and the world turning.

The school – ah, the school. That was where his happy, happy childhood had been formed – where his friendships had been forged. It had been the best of days, and nothing in his later life was ever as brilliant.

He turned the corner into the High Street – the Royal Oak pub, where his grandparents had met their friends on a Friday night, was a beautiful private house now. He supposed that people didn't meet in pubs anymore, the way they once did, there were other ways to socialise now. The Oak had been the first pub he had been taken to, and it had been by his Granddad who had bought him his first beer. Boy, it had tasted good, and he licked his lips as he had done all those years ago.

Up ahead, he could see the Two Brewers. It had changed. It was a sophisticated bar/restaurant now; back then, it was where all the bad boys and girls had hung out. They weren't awful, just young people trying to get a handle on life and enjoying themselves in the process.

He noticed some new houses and some revived old ones nudging the High Street as he continued along. The Cooperative shop had gone – that was where his mother had worked and his Grandmother. It had been an exciting place to hang about, especially at Christmas. He could still remember the smells of that place. The wonderful, beautiful smells.

The allotments were still on the right, still bursting with colours, and plants and love. As he got to the top of Crown Road, it all came rushing back; his pals, the games, the running up and down the road – they were the best, the very best, of times.

The Crown pub hadn't changed, either. This was where he had met the girls and his buddies in his older days. It was a beautiful pub inside and out, and as he thought back, and although his face was sporting a smile, there was still a warm tear on his cheek.

Perhaps the saddest thing is going back, going home and finding that it has changed all too much – but not this place. Coming home to this place was a pleasure. It was a village that had changed little, sure the people were different, and some of the buildings were painted brighter or had been pulled down – but the village was still the village.

He thought he might head over to the school field and look at the place where he had scored that goal – the one which folks had talked about for months. He remembered how everyone in the Royal Oak had bought him a beer because of it. He had played for the village football team but had dreamed of playing, one day, for a big London club. It wasn't to be.

There is a saying that if you want to give God a laugh, tell him what your plans are. Nothing had worked out the way he'd hoped, but he had been luckier than most folks – he had known a place of love, life, and safety. He had the happiest days of his existence in this village and perhaps the saddest days too – but folks had rallied around – everyone had helped, and in the end, he had moved on and moved away.

As he walked towards the school field, he stopped and sat a while outside the village hall. There were worse places to have lived, he thought. He looked over at the little village he had called home, and then he wept. Wept buckets.

For everything and everyone.

THE BEST IS TO COME

Wrap up your soul from the north winds,
Turn your sweet head,
To facing the sun,
I know that those dark clouds will scare you,
But believe me,
The best is to come.

Let slip those stories they told you,
Just remember that you are the one,
Don't let their sadness get weary,
For I tell you,
The best is to come.

Smile 'though the trying is hard work,
Cleanse weary eyes with bright fun,
For these dark days
Will lift soon my darling
And I promise,
The best is to come.

Take strength in the ways of the old times,
When your laughter and hope can return,
Don't stumble and fall,
Take my hand love,
For you know that the best
Is to come.

THE END

It is a strange, sad, and magnificent life,

And although I doubt I would want to do it all again,

I wouldn't have missed any of it for a second,

None of it.

But most of all you.